A New Tune A
for Trombone

Boston Music Company
part of The Music Sales Group
London/New York/Paris/Sydney/Copenhagen/Berlin/Madrid/Tokyo

Foreword

Since its appearance in the early 1930s, C. Paul Herfurth's original *A Tune A Day* series has become the most popular instrumental teaching method of all time. Countless music students have been set on their path by the clear, familiar, proven material, and the logical, sensibly-paced progression through the lessons within the book.

The teacher will find that the new books have been meticulously rewritten by experienced teachers: instrumental techniques and practices have been updated and the musical content has been completely overhauled.

The student will find clearly-presented, uncluttered material, with familiar tunes and a gentle introduction to the theoretical aspects of music. The books are now accompanied by audio CDs of examples and backing tracks to help the student develop a sense of rhythm, intonation and performance at an early stage.

As in the original books, tests are given following every five lessons. Teachers are encouraged to present these as an opportunity to ensure that the student has a good overview of the information studied up to this point.

The following extract from the foreword to the original edition remains as true today as the day it was written:

The value of learning to count aloud from the very beginning cannot be over-estimated. Only in this way can a pupil sense rhythm.

Class teaching should be a combination of individual instruction and ensemble playing. At every lesson there should be individual playing so that all the necessary corrections can be made. Never allow pupils' mistakes to go unnoticed, since only by immediate correction will they develop the habit of careful thinking and playing.

It is recommended that students practise for twenty to thirty minutes a day, as eventual success in mastering the instrument depends on regular and careful home-work.

Music-making is a lifelong pleasure, and at its heart is a solid understanding of the principles of sound production and music theory. These books are designed to accompany the student on these crucial first steps: the rewards for study and practice are immediate and lasting. Welcome to the world of music!

Special thanks to Susie, Sam and Linus

Thanks to Ida and David Miller, Onyx Brass, Ned Bennett, David Stewart, Tim Jackson, Pat Jackman, Duncan Wilson and David Gordon.
Thanks also to The Dulwich Music Shop.

Contents

Published by
Boston Music Company

Exclusive Distributors:
Music Sales Limited
8/9 Frith Street, London W1D 3JB, England.
Music Sales Corporation
257 Park Avenue South, New York, NY10010, USA.
Music Sales Pty Limited
120 Rothschild Avenue, Rosebery, NSW 2018, Australia.

This book © Copyright 2005 & 2006 Boston Music Company,
a division of Music Sales Limited
Revised 2006

Unauthorised reproduction of any part of this publication
by any means including photocopying is an infringement of copyright.

Edited by David Harrison
Music processed by Paul Ewers Music Design
Original compositions and arrangements by Amos Miller
and Ned Bennett
Cover and book designed by Chloë Alexander
Photography by Matthew Ward
Model: Michael May
Printed in the EU
Backing tracks by Guy Dagul
CD performance by Amos Miller
CD recorded, mixed and mastered by Jonas Persson and John Rose

Your Guarantee of Quality
As publishers, we strive to produce every book to the highest commercial
standards. The music has been freshly engraved and the book has been
carefully designed to minimise awkward page turns and to make playing
from it a real pleasure. Throughout, the printing and binding have been
planned to ensure a sturdy, attractive publication which should give years
of enjoyment. If your copy fails to meet our high standards, please inform
us and we will gladly replace it.

www.musicsales.com

Rudiments of music

The stave

Music is written on a grid of five lines called a *stave*.

At the beginning of each stave is placed a special symbol called a *clef* to describe the approximate range of the instrument for which the music is written.

This example shows a *bass clef*, generally used for lower-pitch instruments.

The stave is divided into equal sections of time, called *bars* or *measures*, by *barlines*.

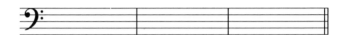

Note values

Different symbols are used to show the time value of *notes*, and each *note value* has an equivalent symbol for a rest, representing silence.

The **quaver** (or *eighth note*), often used to signify a half beat, is written with a solid head and a stem with a tail. The quaver rest is also shown.

The **crotchet** (or *quarter note*), often used to signify one beat, is written with a solid head and a stem. The crotchet rest is also shown.

The **minim** (or *half note*) is worth two crotchets. It is written with a hollow head and a stem. The minim rest is placed on the middle line.

The **semibreve** (or *whole note*) is worth two minims. It is written with a hollow head. The semibreve rest hangs from the fourth line.

Other note values

Note values can be increased by half by adding a dot after the note head. Here a minim and a crotchet are together worth a *dotted* minim.

Grouping quavers

Where two or more quavers follow each other, they can be joined by a *beam* from stem to stem.

Time signatures

The number of beats in a bar is determined by the *time signature*, a pair of numbers placed after the clef.
The upper number shows how many beats each bar contains, whilst the lower number indicates what kind of note value
is used to represent a single beat. This lower number is a fraction of a semibreve so that 4 represents crotchets
and 8 represents quavers.

𝐂, for *common time*, is
another way to write $\frac{4}{4}$.

$\frac{6}{8}$ means six quavers to the bar.

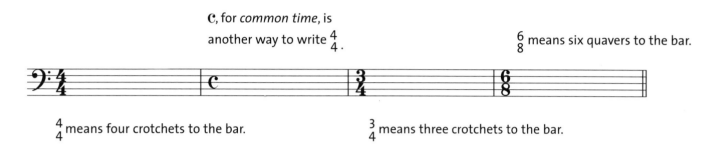

$\frac{4}{4}$ means four crotchets to the bar.

$\frac{3}{4}$ means three crotchets to the bar.

Note names

Notes are named after the first seven letters of the alphabet and are written on lines or spaces on the stave,
according to pitch.

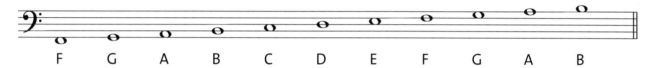

F   G   A   B   C   D   E   F   G   A   B

Accidentals

The pitch of a note can be altered up or down a half step (or *semitone*) by the use of sharp and flat symbols.
These temporary pitch changes are known as accidentals.

The *sharp* (♯) raises the pitch of a note.   The *natural* (♮) returns the note to its original pitch.

The *flat* (♭) lowers the pitch of a note.

Ledger lines

Ledger lines are used to extend the range of the stave for low or high notes.

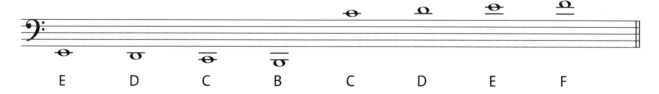

E   D   C   B   C   D   E   F

Bar lines

Various different types of bar lines are used:

Double bar lines divide one section of music from another.   *Final bar* lines show the end of a piece of music.

Repeat marks show a section to be repeated.

Before you play:

Assembling the trombone
Your trombone will be in several pieces.

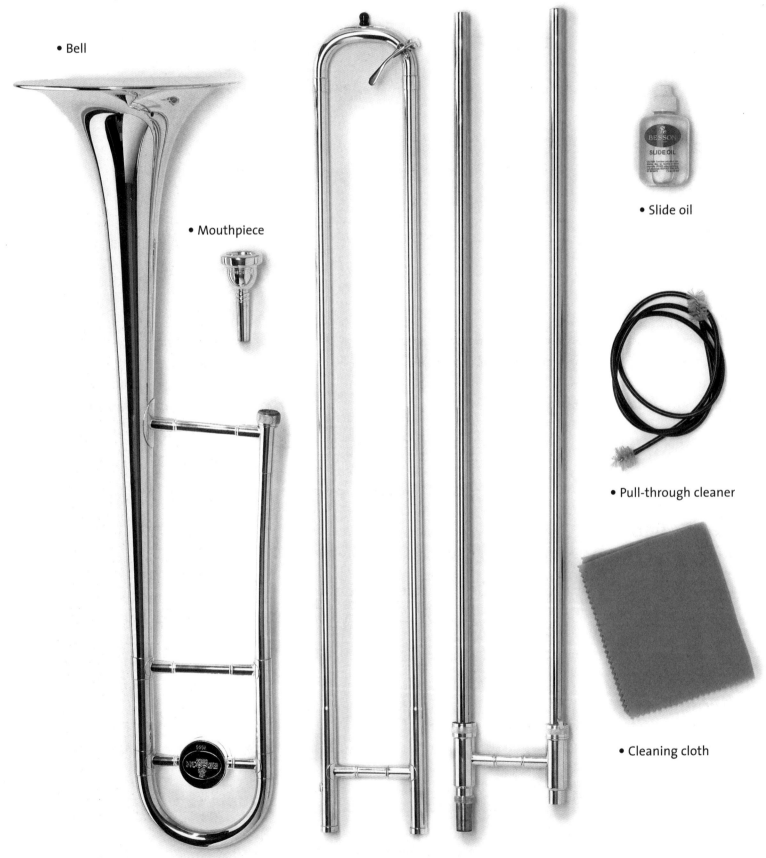

• Bell

• Mouthpiece

• Slide oil

• Pull-through cleaner

• Cleaning cloth

• Outer slide   • Inner slide

Setting-up routine

With the slide assembled, and making sure that the slide lock is on, carefully attach the slide section of the trombone to the bell section using the screw collar. Adjust the angle of the two parts to make a right angle (this can be finely adjusted later, depending on the size of your hand.) Put the mouthpiece into the hole. Do this in reverse to put the trombone away, but make sure you have emptied the condensation out through the water key first.

Be sure to lock the slide when putting the instrument together and when putting it away.

Maintenance

The trombone has fewer complicated components than some other instruments, but nevertheless requires you to be careful when handling it. The slide must be able to move freely and the slightest dent can prevent it from working.

Every two or three days remove the outer slide and place it gently on a flat surface; then wipe the inner slides clean with a soft cloth and reapply a small amount of slide lubricant to the stockings (the raised areas at the bottom). Replace the outer slide carefully, ensuring that the water-key is pointing downwards.

If your trombone is lacquered (ask your teacher if you are not sure), do not polish the instrument using an abrasive metal polish. Warm soapy water and a soft cloth are all that is required. A pull-through brush should be used for both the mouthpiece and slide and for cleaning the insides every two weeks.

Practice

Playing any musical instrument is a physical skill, and repetition is necessary to develop your mental and muscular skills. The three most important things to remember about practice are:

1. Practise until you *can't* get something wrong, rather than just until you get it right once; this way you are less likely to get it wrong next time.

2. It is much better to practise "little and often" rather than in one long session once a week. A daily practice routine of 15 or 20 minutes is ideal.

3. Never finish a practice session without getting at least one thing better than it was when you started.

Lesson 1

goals:

1. **Breathing using the diaphragm**
2. **Posture and instrument position**
3. **Formation of the *embouchure* or mouth position**
4. **Tonguing**
5. **The notes F, B♭ and D**
6. **Counting while playing semibreves, minims and crotchets**

Breathing

Always remember to breathe through your mouth when playing the trombone.

When breathing in and out, always use your diaphragm. This is a large dome-shaped muscular membrane underneath your rib cage that draws the lungs open when you breathe in and lets them close as you breathe out.

As it draws the lungs open it flattens and gets bigger which means that your stomach goes *outwards* as you breathe in, and *inwards* as you breathe out.

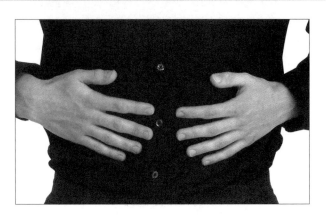

Exercise 1:

Breathe in whilst counting four even beats, and then breathe out whilst counting 4 and so on.
Keep the speed of the air in and out steady, using the diaphragm to control it.

in 2 3 4   out 2 3 4   in 2 3 4   out 2 3 4   in 2 3 4   out 2 3 4   in 2 3 4   out 2 3 4

Place a hand on your stomach to check whether it is going *out* as you breathe *in*, and *in* when you breathe *out*.

Posture and instrument position

Playing the trombone is a physical activity! It is important that you keep yourself fit for the task by making sure that you stand up straight with your feet flat on the floor and slightly apart.

Imagine a string from the ceiling to the top of your head taking almost all your weight, so you feel light and ready for action.

Left hand grip

Make the shape of a pistol pointing in the air with your left hand: thumb out, index finger up and the other three fingers curled round.

Right hand position

Hold the slide with the right hand, gripping the outer stay gently between thumb and fingers, with two fingers above, and two below, the bottom of the outer slide. Now put the instrument to your lips, remembering always to keep your head upright.

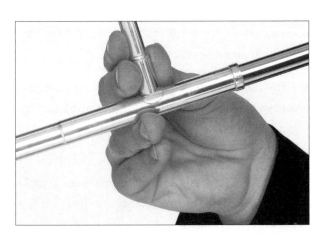

Embouchure

The mouthpiece should rest on the centre point of the mouth, approximately two thirds on the top lip, and one third on the bottom. (This assumes that you have a standard 'overbite', where your top teeth are in front of the bottom when your mouth is closed.)

The corners of the mouth should feel as if they 'grip' the mouthpiece, allowing the lips themselves to vibrate. Your mouth shouldn't feel stretched in either a 'smiley' or a 'droopy' way, as this will stop the lips vibrating so well. Imagine the lips as an elastic band stretched between two matchsticks.

Remember to check the mouthpiece position with your teacher, or use a mirror at home. Don't puff out your cheeks!

Those with larger hands may find it easier to place the top stay between the middle and ring fingers.

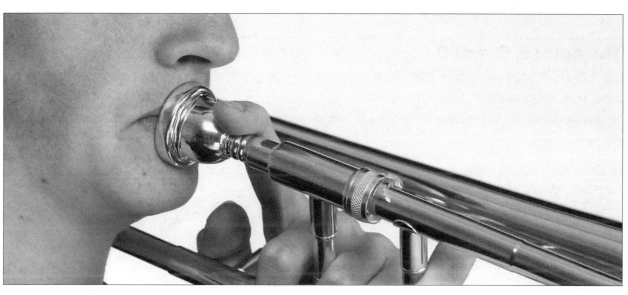

Exercise 2:

Try this with just the mouthpiece to make a 'buzzing' sound and then with the mouthpiece in the trombone.

Breathe · Buzz · Breathe · Buzz · Breathe · Buzz

Tonguing

Sound is made on the trombone by blowing air through the lips and making them vibrate. The tongue provides a clean beginning to the notes, and the trombone amplifies the sound made in the mouthpiece.

Try saying the word **Too** a few times. Can you feel where your tongue is as you start the word? The tip of the tongue should be at the point behind your top teeth where your teeth join the roof of your mouth and this is exactly where the tongue should be at the start of a note.

Exercise 3:

Breathe · 'Too' · Breathe · 'Too' · Breathe · 'Too'

Compare first position with 4th position in the image above.

The notes F, B♭ and D

F and B♭ are in first position (the slide all the way in) and D is in fourth position (the collar at the top of the outer slide is approximately level with the bell).

To change from the F to the lower B♭ in first position, it can be helpful to let the bottom jaw move down and forward a little.

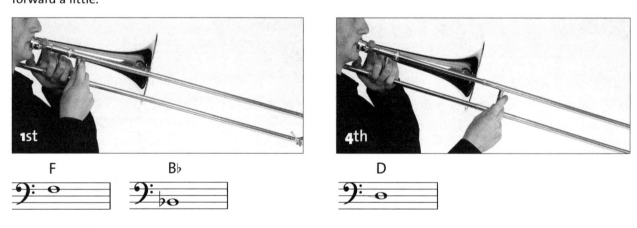

F   B♭   D

Exercise 4:

Remember to breathe during the rests as well as at the beginning. The notes are semibreves, worth four beats.

Exercise 5:

The notes and rests here are called minims, worth two beats each.

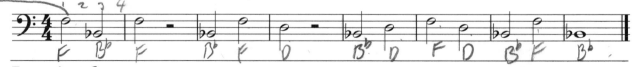

Exercise 6:

These notes and rests are called crotchets, which are worth one beat each. These rests are shorter than in the previous exercises, so be sure to breathe quickly.

10

Pieces for Lesson 1

The Lewisham Stomp

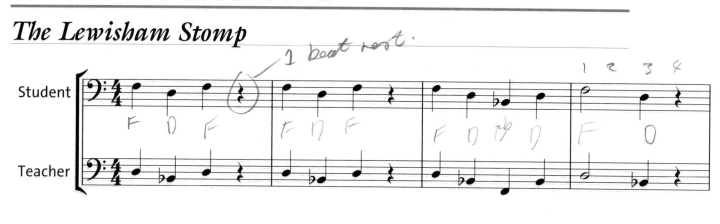

Spring Has Sprung

Fanfare

1. **The notes C and E♭**
2. **Breathing with an open throat**
3. **Dotted minims**
4. **Three beats per bar**

The note C

C

The note E♭

E♭

Exercise 1:

The symbol above the notes here is called a **pause**.

This means you should hold the note for longer than its usual value.

3rd position

E♭ B♭ E♭ B♭ F B♭

OPENING YOUR THROAT

A quick way to find out what an open throat feels like is to yawn!

Blow on the back of your hand. You will feel the air is cold.
Now try again, pretending that you are steaming up a window.
This time the air on the back of your hand should feel warm because you have just breathed out with your throat open. You should keep your throat open at all times when playing as it will improve your tone.

Exercise 2:

Play these notes with an open throat. The **'** above is a breath mark to indicate where you should breathe. Take a *quick* breath here (imagine you have just touched a hot iron!) without disturbing the 4 beats/bar counting.

Dotted notes

A dot just following a note increases its length by half.

For example, a minim with a dot would increase in length from 2 beats to 3:

Exercise 3:

Count carefully as you play these notes, remembering to keep an open throat.

Make sure the rests are the right length too.

Time signatures

Everything you have played so far has had a **time signature** of four beats to every bar:

1, 2, 3, 4, **1**, 2, 3, 4, **1**, 2, 3, 4 etc.

Many pieces, however, contain three beats per bar.

This means that the counting will be: **1**, 2, 3, **1**, 2, 3, **1**, 2, 3 etc.

Waltzes always use this time signature.

Exercise 4:

Count 3 beats in every bar.

Did you notice the two dots at the end before the last bar line?

This is called a repeat sign and means 'play the section again'.

13

Pieces for Lesson 2

Barcarolle

Offenbach

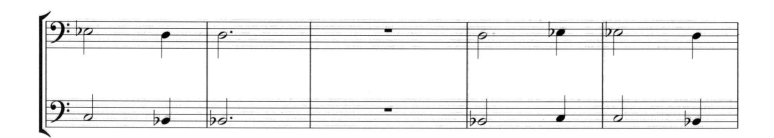

Medieval Dance

Pieces for Lesson 2

Jingle Bells

Now The Day Is Over

Merrily

Back To Bed

Lesson **3** goals:
1. **The note G**
2. **Developing good slide technique**
3. **Breathing in time**

The note G

4th

G

Exercise 1:

Ensure that you move the slide quickly to keep the count steady, even when moving the slide a long way.
Begin this exercise slowly and speed it up as your coordination improves.

*Keep the notes
crisp and clean.*

Exercise 2:

*Ensure that
the breath, tongue
and slide all
work together.*

F G F D F

Breathing in time

It's very important not to lose your place in a piece of music, and to help you to start a piece of music in the
right way it's a good idea to count in silently before playing.

If the piece has 4 beats to the bar try counting 'one, two, three' to yourself and take a breath on the 4th beat.

Exercise 3:

*Take care not to
mix up lines or spaces.*

Pieces for Lesson 3

Twinkle, Twinkle Little Star

Oats And Beans

Lightly Row

1. **The note low A**
2. **Ties and slurs**

The note low A

2nd

A

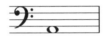

Ties and slurs

These are curved lines that are used to join notes together.

A tie is used to join two notes of the same pitch and a slur joins notes of two different pitches:

2nd   2nd   2   1

Exercise 1:

The ties are used to carry the note over into the next bar. Count very carefully.

1 6 4 3

Exercise 2:

Slurs are used to make music smoother: if you want to play some gentle pieces, tonguing every note with a "too" sound can make the music a bit spiky!

On the trombone some notes can be slurred without tonguing at all, whilst between others a soft 'doo' sound is needed.

Only the first note of each pair should be tongued here.

Exercise 3:

These slurs need a very soft tongue.

Make sure the slide moves quickly to keep the notes clean.

Pieces for Lesson 4

Largo (from the New World Symphony)

Dvořák **13–14**

Susie's Waltz

15–16

Steal Away

Spiritual **17–18**

Canon For Two

The second player starts one bar after the first.

The note low G

Dynamics

Notes and rhythms are two of the elements of music, but without expression, music can be lifeless and mechanical. One of the obvious ways of introducing *colour* into music is to play sections of pieces or phrases at different levels of loudness. Here are a couple of Italian terms commonly used:

f stands for the word *forte* and means loud.   *p* stands for the word *piano* which means quiet.

Exercise 1:

Play these notes at the dynamic that is written underneath. To play louder, use the diaphragm to push the air through the instrument faster. Slow the air flow down to play quietly.

Exercise 2:

The $\mathbf{c}$ at the start is an alternative way of writing the time signature $\frac{4}{4}$ and is called '**Common Time**'.

Try not to confuse C, E♭ and G – they are all written in spaces.

Exercise 3:

Start slowly with this tricky piece, and try to play it a little faster each time you practise it.

Pieces for Lesson 5

When The Saints

London Bridge Is Falling Down (adapted)

Joshua Fought The Battle Of Jericho

Spiritual

Lesson 5

Warm-up

Here's a short warm-up routine to prepare you for your practice sessions, in the same way an athlete would.

1   Blow a few raspberries and feel your lips flap about nice and loosely.

2   Using the mouthpiece alone, do some 'buzzing'. Take a big breath and sound like an angry bee!
Try this: the wavy lines indicate a sliding sound or *glissando*.

3   Replace the mouthpiece and blow air through the instrument without making a sound – as if you are steaming up the inside of the instrument with nice warm air, and imagine a beautiful trombone sound.

4   Play an F.

Try to match that beautiful sound you were imagining.

5   Play some gentle slurs. As you slur downwards, imagine you are a hippo sitting down slowly on a sofa!
This will help get a lovely warm sound on the lower note. As you slur upwards your diaphragm needs to give a little extra push to help the hippo up again.
Play these two exercises in each position from 1 to 4.

This whole warm-up should only take a few minutes.
Make it a regular part of your practice routine to help you develop a good technique.

GOOD HABITS

1 Stand up straight,
with your feet flat on the floor.

2 Breathe deeply, using the
diaphragm, and without raising
the shoulders.

3 Count while you play
and breathe in time.

4 Put the trombone to your mouth,
not your mouth to the trombone.

1. Note values

On the stave below, draw notes of the length indicated:

| 4 beats | 2 beats | 1 beat | 3 beats |

(4)

2. Rests

On the stave below, draw rests of the length indicated:

| 4 beats | 2 beats | 1 beat | 3 beats |

(4)

3. Notes

On the stave below, draw the following notes as minims:

F, B♭, D, C, E♭, G, low A and **low G**

(8)

4. How many notes?

Count how many notes you would hear if you were listening to this.

(2)

5. Bars

Draw bar lines on this stave where they are needed.

(7)

Total (25)

Lesson 6

goals:

1. The note E natural (E♮)
2. Key signatures
3. Quavers

The note E ♮

2nd

E natural

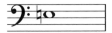

E♮ comes between E♭ and F which are a tone apart. E♮ is a **semitone** away from both these notes.

A semitone is the smallest distance – or interval – that is used in most Western music.

Exercise 1:

Listen to how close E♮ sounds to its neighbours F and E♭.

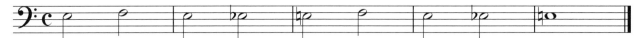

Exercise 2:

These notes are much further apart.

Play this as neatly as you can.

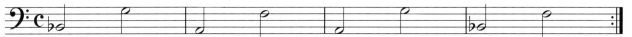

Key signatures

If you try to sing a simple tune with a big range such as *The Star Spangled Banner*, you may find early on that you can't reach the high notes without straining. The solution is to start the piece a little lower.

This time, you may be able to sing the high notes perfectly. You are now singing the piece in a different **key**.

Music has many keys, and each needs its own set of notes. **C major** is easy to remember as it has no sharps or flats (all the white notes on a piano). The key of **F major** requires all the **B**s to be played as **B♭**. The key of **B♭** major requires all the **B**s and **E**s to be played as **B♭** and **E♭**. These alterations are shown at the beginning of each stave as the **key signature**.

F major

B♭ major

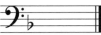

Exercise 3:

You have already learned this famous tune. Try the first two bars in C major and then again in B♭ major. Notice that the key signature of B♭ major tells you that all the Es and Bs are actually E♭s and B♭s otherwise the tune will sound wrong.

Bell

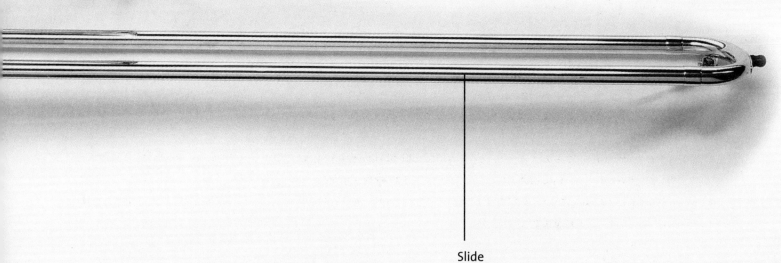

Slide

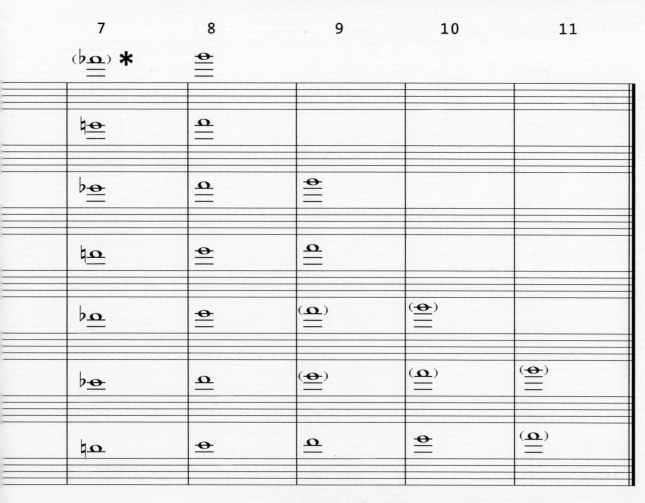

✱ Notes played with the 7th harmonic are flat, and positions should be shortened accordingly. The note A♭ in 1st position should for this reason be avoided.

Tuning Slide

Slide Lock Ring

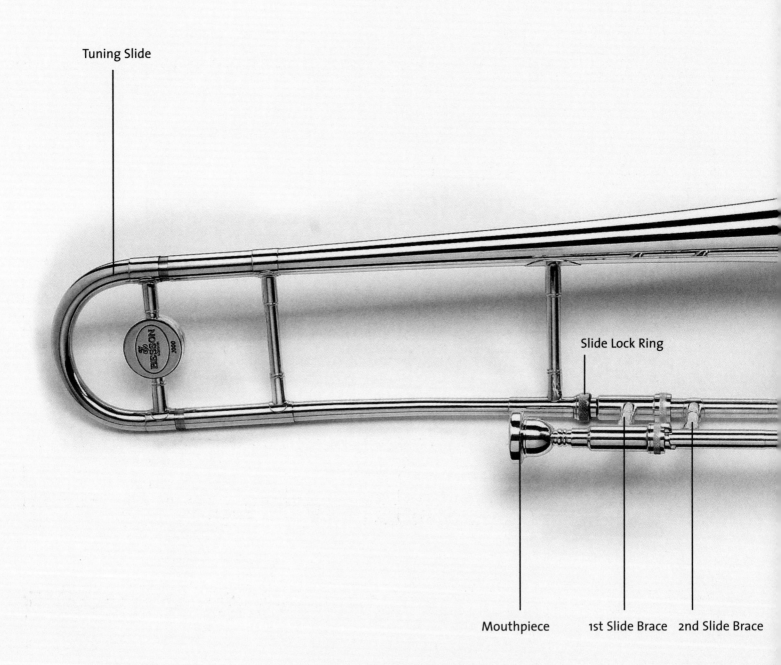

Mouthpiece

1st Slide Brace

2nd Slide Brace

Quavers

Single quavers and a quaver rest

Quavers in pairs
(worth 1 crotchet per pair)

Quavers as a group
(a minim's worth)

Exercise 4:

The note values in the first four bars halve from one bar to the next .

Count carefully and play to a steady beat.

Quavers last for half as long as crotchets.

Pieces for Lesson 6

Abide With Me

This Old Man

25–26

Lesson 7

goals:

1. **The note upper A♭**
2. **Dotted crotchets**
3. **Tempo and character marking**
4. **Upbeats**

The note upper A♭

Dotted crotchets

In the same way that the length of a minim was increased by half in lesson 2, a dot after a crotchet has the same effect. A dot following a crotchet increases its value from two quavers to three.

Exercise 1:

Play this slowly so that you can count each quaver. The more you practise the more you will find that you will be able to recognise patterns of rhythms and notes without having to read each note individually.

Exercise 2:

Now try this pattern with three beats in each bar. Notice the quaver rest in the fourth bar.

Use the quaver rest to take a breath.

Tempo and character markings

Composers often provide words at the beginning of a piece of music to show the style and tempo that the piece should be played. Try to play the following pieces in the style and at the speed indicated.

Up-beats

Sometimes a piece of music doesn't begin with a whole bar.

Go Down Moses starts with a single beat representing the last beat of a bar. This short bar at the beginning is 'made up' at the end of the piece with a bar worth the remainder of the up-beat bar.

The short bar at the beginning of a piece of music is sometimes referred to as an *anacrusis*.

Pieces for Lesson 7

Go Down Moses

Spiritual

27–28

Hymn

From *The Unfinished Symphony*

Schubert

29–30

This piece has six beats to the bar. Watch out for the E♮ s!

Betty's Biscuits

31–32

goals:

1. The notes upper B♭ and upper A
2. The scale of B♭ major
3. DC al Fine

The note upper B♭

1st

B♭

The note upper A

2nd

A

Exercise 1:

Compare the sounds of the low B♭ with the upper B♭ and the low A with the upper A. Are they in tune?

The scale of B♭ major

The notes of the major scale follow a particular pattern of intervals.

Most of the notes are a tone apart, but between the 3rd and 4th notes of the scale, and again between the 7th and 8th notes of the scale, the interval is only half as much: a semitone.

| Tone | Tone | Semitone | Tone | Tone | Tone | Semitone |

1   2   3   4   5   6   7   8

Exercise 2:

Try to make sure the notes of the scale are all played evenly; and that the tone is consistent throughout.

DC al Fine

This Italian expression literally means 'from the beginning' (*da capo*) to the end (*Fine*).

In the *Skye Boat Song*, play the repeated section, and then begin the piece again, playing through until you reach the *fine*, which is the end of the piece.

Pieces for Lesson 8

Skye Boat Song

Scottish traditional

The Can Can

Offenbach

Grandfather's Clock

Kookaburra (a round)

A new player can begin every two bars.

Lesson 9 goals:

1. The note low A♭
2. The scale of A♭ major
3. More dynamics

The note low A♭

A♭

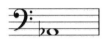

The scale of A♭ major

When we played B♭ major in the last lesson we played all the notes tongued.

This time, see how smoothly you can play it. Playing all the notes slurred like this is called *legato*.

Make sure your tongue makes a **doo** sound and remember to move your slide quickly and smoothly between notes.

Exercise 1:

More dynamics

So far we have only learned two dynamics, soft (***p***) and loud (***f***). The letter ***m*** can be used in combination with ***p*** and ***f*** to create other dynamics: ***mp*** (*mezzo piano*) means moderately soft and ***mf*** (*mezzo forte*) means moderately loud. The Italian word *mezzo* means literally 'half'.

Exercise 2:

Play these notes with the marked dynamics.

*Try to keep your dynamics consistent. Are all the **f**'s the same? And the **p**'s?*

f   ***mf***   ***mp***   ***p***   ***p***   ***mp***   ***mf***   ***f***   ***f***

Pieces for Lesson 9

Oh Come All Ye Faithful

 39–40

Good King Wenceslas

41–42

The First Noël

43–44

1. **The notes upper C and upper B natural (B♮)**
2. **The scale of C major**
3. **Triplets and the 6/8 time signature**

The note upper C

3rd

C

The note upper B♮

4th

B natural

The Scale of C major

Keep the air flowing all the way through the scale. Start slowly and get faster as you become more comfortable with the notes. Aim to play the whole scale up and down in one breath.

Triplets

Crotchets divided in two make quavers. Sometimes it is necessary to divide the beat into three. These are called called **triplets**.

Exercise 1:

Make sure that the quavers are nice and even.

Every group of 3 triplets in exercise 2 has a small '3' above or below it.

If a piece of music has lots of triplets in it the time signature of $\frac{6}{8}$ can be used: this has two beats per bar, but each beat is three quavers long. Notice how a single beat is now shown as a dotted crotchet, rather than the more usual crotchet.

Here is the same exercise again, but this time written out in $\frac{6}{8}$

Exercise 2:

Pieces for Lesson 10

Lullaby

Brahms

45-46

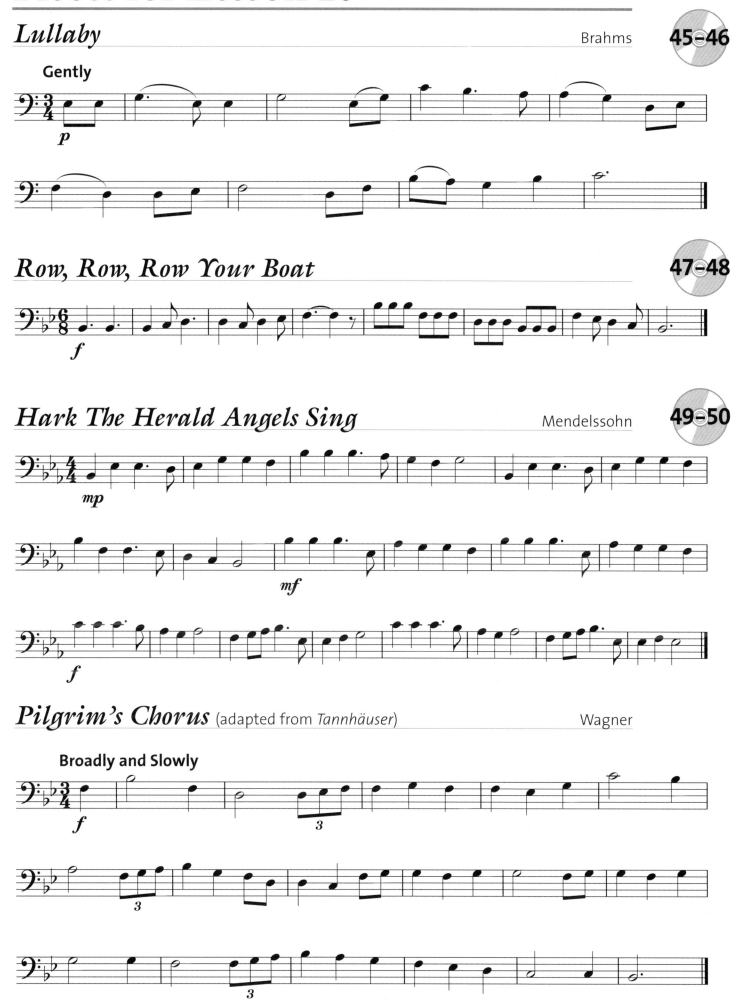

Row, Row, Row Your Boat

47-48

Hark The Herald Angels Sing

Mendelssohn

49-50

Pilgrim's Chorus (adapted from *Tannhäuser*)

Wagner

Broadly and Slowly

Pieces for Lesson 10

Learn both lines for duet playing. The melody is on the top line.

Spring (from the *Four Seasons*)

Vivaldi

Briskly

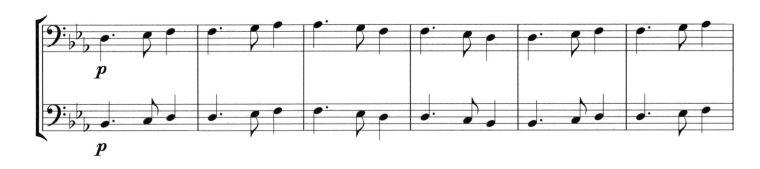

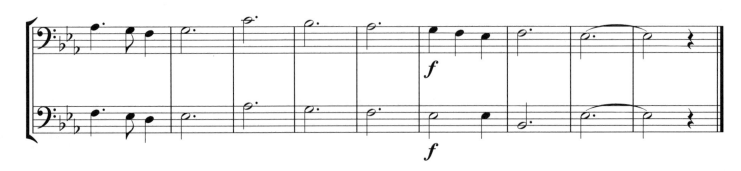

1. Note Lengths

On the stave below write notes of the indicated length:

| One quaver | A minim's worth of quavers | A dotted crotchet | A note lasting five quavers |

(8)

2. Scale

On the stave below write the scale of A♭ major including the correct key signature:

(4)

3. Notes

On the stave below draw the following notes as crotchets:

E♮, upper A, B♭, B♮ and C

(4)

4. Dynamics

What are the Italian words for the following? How are they abbreviated?

Moderately loud _____

Moderately soft _____

(4)

5. Naming names

Identify all the items indicated by the arrows:

p

(5)

Total **(25)**

Lesson 11 goals:

1. The note D♭
2. Staccato
3. Minor keys
4. The scale of C minor
5. Accidentals

The note D♭

D♭

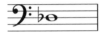

Staccato

Notes marked with a dot above them are played staccato, or very detached.

Staccato notes should be played shorter than usual, with an audible gap between the notes.

Exercise 1:

Play this melody in a staccato style.

Don't be tempted to hurry just because the notes are shorter than usual.

Minor keys

Most of the pieces studied so far have been in a **major** key, and have a happy, outgoing sound.

Pieces with a sadder, more reflective feel are often written in a **minor** key.

Exercise 2:

Revise the C major scale you learned in the last lesson, and listen to the bright character of the scale.

Exercise 3: the C minor scale

Listen to the sound of the minor scale and compare it with the bright major version.

This scale starts on the same note, C, but uses a different set of notes.

Notice how the key signature now has three flats, B♭, E♭ and A♭. In fact, in this version of the minor scale, the harmonic minor, the seventh note is raised by a semitone. For this reason the scale includes B♮.

Where correcting symbols appear in the music they are known as *accidentals*.

Pieces for Lesson 11

Oh! Susannah

Hava Nagila

Israeli traditional

Auld Lang Syne

goals:

1. **The note upper D**
2. *Crescendo* and *diminuendo*
3. **The scale of D minor**

The note upper D

Crescendo and diminuendo

All dynamic changes you have played so far have been instant. However, suddenly changing from *piano* to *forte* has a different impact from a gradual change.

Crescendo means becoming gradually louder, also shown as:

Diminuendo means becoming gradually quieter, also shown as:

Exercise 1:

Play these long notes for the correct number of beats, taking care to pace the *crescendi* and *diminuendi* to make them smooth.

Remember to take big breaths so that you don't run out of air.

The Scale of D minor

Watch out for the accidentals in this scale, and be sure to play the scale as a melody.

Exercise 2:

Pieces for Lesson 12

Scarborough Fair

English traditional

Swing Low, Sweet Chariot

Spiritual

Ode To Joy (from *Symphony no.9*)

Beethoven

Lesson 13 goals:

1. **The notes G♭ and upper D♭**
2. **Enharmonic notes**

The notes G♭ and upper D♭

Enharmonic notes

From previous lessons, you will know that A♭ is a semitone *below* A, and at the same time a semitone *above* G.

This means that the same note could be called G♯. These two notes are *enharmonic equivalents*.

Similarly the G♭ above could be called F♯, and the D♭ above could be called C♯.

Exercise 1:

Play the following notes. You have already studied the enharmonic equivalents.

Exercise 2:

These two short pieces need the note you have just learnt, the first time as D♭, the second as C♯.

You should also spot two other enharmonic differences. Don't panic, these two pieces sound exactly the same!

The following two pieces are indentical, except that one uses flats and the other uses the sharp equivalents.

The last piece on the opposite page, *Greensleeves*, has five flats.

Play these all through to familiarise yourself with them before you start the piece.

Pieces for Lesson 13

Silent Night

Grüber

62-63

Devil's Laughter (from Caprice no.13)

Paganini

Greensleeves

Attributed to Henry VIII

64-65

Lesson 14 goals:

1. **Swing quavers**
2. **Playing jazz**

Swing

In classical music, quavers are played exactly as written and last exactly half the length of a crotchet.

In jazz, however, quavers are usually played in an uneven way: the first quaver of each pair takes longer than half a beat and the second is shorter. This is known as **swing**, and will be indicated in the music.

Exercise 1:

Try saying **tutu tutu tutu tutu**, making sure each syllable is completely even:
this is the rhythm of quavers in classical music.

Now try saying **dooby dooby dooby dooby** and notice how it swings along.
This is the rhythm of quavers in swing music.

Swing quavers have a bouncing feel to them. This is because the second syllable is a bit shorter that the first, like a shorter second quaver of the pair.

Exercise 2:

Play this B♭ major scale in a swing rhythm. Try it first tongued and then with the slurs as marked.

Exercise 3:

'If You're Happy And You Know It' is a famous example of a tune that swings.

42

Pieces for Lesson 14

Little Brown Jug

Traditional

Joshua Jazz

Blooz For Sooz

goals:

1. **Scales and arpeggios**
2. **Some Italian terms**

Scales

If you look at the pieces in this book you will find that the melodies are generally made from fragments of scales and arpeggios.

Familiarity with scales and arpeggios will help you to play these melodies more confidently and smoothly.

It is very important to practise scales: they help to train muscle memory.

Regular practice will help you train your muscles to respond to different keys without having to think, as well as helping your breath control, intonation and range.

Arpeggios are built from the 1st, 3rd and 5th notes of a scale, and are very useful as practice exercises. Here are arpeggios from some of the scales studied so far.

Remember to play them both slurred and tongued.

C major

A♭ major

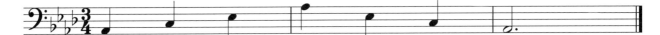

C minor

D minor

More Italian words

In addition to dynamics, composers often use Italian words to indicate the speed (*tempo*) or the style of the piece. Here are some of the more common terms:

Allegro Quickly	**Moderato** Moderately	**Andante** At a walking pace
Adagio Slowly	**Accelerando** (accel.) Becoming faster	**Rallentando** (rall.) Becoming slower
Dolce Sweetly	**Cantabile** In a singing style	

The big slur marks in the following piece indicates phrases, and connect notes together much as words in a sentence would be. Where possible, each phrase should be played in a single breath.

Pieces for Lesson 15

Danny Boy

Irish traditional

Play this piece as smoothly as possible, in a cantabile style.

Mango Walk

Jamaican traditional

DS al Fine is very much like the *DC al Fine* studied in Lesson 8.

However instead of playing from the beginning (*da capo*) this piece is played from another point in the piece shown by a sign (*DS*, or *dal segno*, means 'from the sign'). You will see the sign 𝄋 above the first bar line.

Fine indicates the actual end of the piece.

Pieces for Lesson 15

Befiehl Du Deine Wege (adapted)

J.S.Bach

Adagio cantabile

test: *for* Lessons 11 to 15

1. Key signatures

On the stave below, draw the correct key signatures for:

B♭ major   C major   A♭ minor   A♭ minor   C minor

(5)

2. Dots

Simplify the music on the left by using dots to replace ties:

(5)

3. Notes

On the stave below draw the following notes as crotchets:

Upper D, D♭, low G and **low A♭**

(6)

4. Italian terms

What do the following terms mean:

Allegro _____

Andante _____

Dolce _____

Cantabile _____

(4)

5. Naming names

Identify all the items indicated by arrows

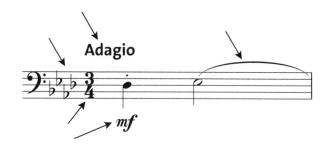

(5)

Total **(25)**

47

CD backing tracks

1 Tuning Note Low B♭
2 Virtuoso Performance
3 Fanfare *demonstration*
4 Fanfare *backing only*
5 Berceuse *teacher part*
6 Medieval Dance *teacher part*
7 Jingle Bells *demonstration*
8 Jingle Bells *backing only*
9 Merrily *demonstration*
10 Merrily *backing only*
11 Twinkle Twinkle Little Star *demonstration*
12 Twinkle Twinkle Little Star *backing only*
13 Largo (from The New World Symphony) *demonstration*
14 Largo (from The New World Symphony) *backing only*
15 Susie's Waltz *demonstration*
16 Susie's Waltz *backing only*
17 Steal Away *demonstration*
18 Steal Away *backing only*
19 When The Saints Go Marching In *demonstration*
20 When The Saints Go Marching In *backing only*
21 London Bridge Is Falling Down *demonstration*
22 London Bridge is Falling Down *backing only*
23 Joshua Fought The Battle Of Jericho *demonstration*
24 Joshua Fought The Battle Of Jericho *backing only*
25 This Old Man *demonstration*
26 This Old Man *backing only*
27 Go Down Moses *demonstration*
28 Go Down Moses *backing only*

29 The Unfinished Symphony *demonstration*
30 The Unfinished Symphony *backing only*
31 Betty's Biscuits *demonstration*
32 Betty's Biscuits *backing only*
33 Skye Boat Song *demonstration*
34 Skye Boat Song *backing only*
35 The Can Can *demonstration*
36 The Can Can *backing only*
37 Grandfather's Clock *demonstration*
38 Grandfather's Clock *backing only*
39 Oh Come All Ye Faithful *demonstration*
40 Oh Come All Ye Faithful *backing only*
41 Good King Wenceslas *demonstration*
42 Good King Wenceslas *backing only*
43 The First Noel *demonstration*
44 The First Noel *backing only*
45 Lullaby *demonstration*
46 Lullaby *backing only*
47 Row, Row, Row Your Boat *demonstration*
48 Row, Row, Row Your Boat *backing only*
49 Hark The Herald Angels Sing *demonstration*
50 Hark The Herald Angels Sing *backing only*
51 Oh! Susannah *demonstration*
52 Oh! Susannah *backing only*
53 Hava Nagila *demonstration*
54 Hava Nagila *backing only*
55 Auld Lang Syne *demonstration*
56 Auld Lang Syne *backing only*

57 Scarborough Fair (duet)
58 Swing Low. Sweet Chariot *demonstration*
59 Swing Low. Sweet Chariot *backing only*
60 Ode To Joy *demonstration*
61 Ode To Joy *backing only*
62 Silent Night *demonstration*
63 Silent Night *backing only*
64 Greensleeves *demonstration*
65 Greensleeves *backing only*
66 Little Brown Jug *demonstration*
67 Little Brown Jug *backing only*
68 Joshua Jazz *demonstration*
69 Joshua Jazz *backing only*
70 Blooz for Sooz *demonstration*
71 Blooz for Sooz *backing only*
72 Danny Boy *demonstration*
73 Danny Boy *backing only*
74 Mango Walk *demonstration*
75 Mango Walk *backing only*

How to use the CD

The tuning note on track 1 is low B♭.

After track 2, which gives an idea of how the trombone can sound, the backing tracks are listed in the order in which they appear in the book.

Look for the 💿 symbol in the book for the relevant backing track. Where both parts of a duet are included on the CD, the top part is in the left channel, and the bottom part is in the right channel.

23456789